T0247179

TRENDS IN SOUTHEAST ASIA

The **ISEAS – Yusof Ishak Institute** (formerly Institute of Southeast Asian Studies) is an autonomous organization established in 1968. It is a regional centre dedicated to the study of socio-political, security, and economic trends and developments in Southeast Asia and its wider geostrategic and economic environment. The Institute's research programmes are grouped under Regional Economic Studies (RES), Regional Strategic and Political Studies (RSPS), and Regional Social and Cultural Studies (RSCS). The Institute is also home to the ASEAN Studies Centre (ASC), the Singapore APEC Study Centre and the Temasek History Research Centre (THRC).

ISEAS Publishing, an established academic press, has issued more than 2,000 books and journals. It is the largest scholarly publisher of research about Southeast Asia from within the region. ISEAS Publishing works with many other academic and trade publishers and distributors to disseminate important research and analyses from and about Southeast Asia to the rest of the world.

UNDERSTANDING AND REDUCING METHANE EMISSIONS IN SOUTHEAST ASIA

Qiu Jiahui and Ryan Wong

ISSUE
8
2022

Published by: ISEAS Publishing
30 Heng Mui Keng Terrace
Singapore 119614
publish@iseas.edu.sg
http://bookshop.iseas.edu.sg

ISEAS Library Cataloguing-in-Publication Data

Name(s): Qiu, Jiahui, author. | Wong, Yee Yang Ryan, author.
Title: Understanding and reducing methane emissions in Southeast Asia / by Qiu Jiahui and Ryan Wong.
Description: Singapore : ISEAS-Yusof Ishak Institute, May 2022. | Series: Trends in Southeast Asia, ISSN 0219-3213 ; TRS8/22 | Includes bibliographical references.
Identifiers: ISBN 9789815011524 (soft cover) | ISBN 9789815011531 (pdf)
Subjects: LCSH: Methane—Environmental aspects—Southeast Asia.
Classification: LCC DS501 I59T no. 8(2022)

Typeset by Superskill Graphics Pte Ltd
Printed in Singapore by Mainland Press Pte Ltd

FOREWORD

The economic, political, strategic and cultural dynamism in Southeast Asia has gained added relevance in recent years with the spectacular rise of giant economies in East and South Asia. This has drawn greater attention to the region and to the enhanced role it now plays in international relations and global economics.

The sustained effort made by Southeast Asian nations since 1967 towards a peaceful and gradual integration of their economies has had indubitable success, and perhaps as a consequence of this, most of these countries are undergoing deep political and social changes domestically and are constructing innovative solutions to meet new international challenges. Big Power tensions continue to be played out in the neighbourhood despite the tradition of neutrality exercised by the Association of Southeast Asian Nations (ASEAN).

The **Trends in Southeast Asia** series acts as a platform for serious analyses by selected authors who are experts in their fields. It is aimed at encouraging policymakers and scholars to contemplate the diversity and dynamism of this exciting region.

THE EDITORS

Series Chairman:
  Choi Shing Kwok

Series Editor:
  Ooi Kee Beng

Editorial Committee:
  Daljit Singh
  Francis E. Hutchinson
  Norshahril Saat

Understanding and Reducing Methane Emissions in Southeast Asia

By Qiu Jiahui and Ryan Wong

EXECUTIVE SUMMARY

- A few ASEAN countries have signed the Global Methane Pledge, but methane should receive a broader and higher priority from the entire region, given its significant contribution to climate change, and the availability of solutions.
- The agriculture sector contributes the most amount of methane emissions with a steadily rising share over the past decade.
- Several Southeast Asian countries face similar methane abatement challenges (i.e., agricultural productivity in Vietnam, Thailand, Myanmar and the Philippines; gas leakage in Malaysia and Brunei; and waste management in Indonesia, Malaysia and Singapore), warranting closer collaboration at the subregional level.
- While it is true that countries have been participating in international initiatives and implementing national policies related to rice cultivation and oil and gas processing, their impacts have not been thoroughly evaluated.
- Rather than creating new institutional structures, ASEAN could for example ensure that its existing working groups and networks prioritize methane abatement.
- Missing data on the relative contribution to methane emissions from livestock, rice paddies and informal economies should be collected to help refine problem definition and formulate effective solutions.

Understanding and Reducing Methane Emissions in Southeast Asia

By Qiu Jiahui and Ryan Wong[1]

INTRODUCTION

The Global Methane Pledge was ratified at the end of 2021. While intense discussion of its significance dominated the climate discourse in North America and Europe, the reception of the Pledge in Southeast Asia was lukewarm. This paper aims to help the policy community understand four major aspects concerning methane emissions: basic science, global ambition, regional trends, and sector challenges.

In 1990, the Intergovernmental Panel on Climate Change (IPCC) published its First Assessment Report, in which scientists stated with certainty that human-caused greenhouse gases were accumulating in the atmosphere. One of these significant gases was methane.[2] Since then, global methane emissions have increased by 17.4 per cent, reaching 8.3 billion tCO2e in 2018.[3] Unlike carbon dioxide, which can persist in the atmosphere for hundreds of years, methane only lasts around 12–15 years before being broken down. Despite being emitted in smaller amounts, methane is a highly potent greenhouse gas compared to carbon dioxide. In fact, methane has been responsible for about 30 per cent

---

[1] Qiu Jiahui is Research Officer in the Climate Change in Southeast Asia Programme at the ISEAS – Yusof Ishak Institute, Singapore; Ryan Wong was Lead Researcher (Energy) in the same programme.

[2] IPCC and WMO, eds., *Climate Change: The 1990 and 1992 IPCC Assessments, IPCC First Assessment Report Overview and Policymaker Summaries and 1992 IPPC Supplement* (Geneva: IPCC, 1992).

[3] Hannah Ritchie and Max Roser, "CO_2 and Greenhouse Gas Emissions", *Our World in Data*, 11 May 2020, https://ourworldindata.org/greenhouse-gas-emissions

of global temperature rise since the industrial revolution.[4] Its relative potency is measured by its Global Warming Potential (GWP), a metric that reflects the global warming impact of each type of greenhouse gas relative to carbon dioxide over a particular time period. Over a period of 100 years, methane has a GWP of 27.9[5]—that is, 1 kg of methane has the same warming impact as 27.9 kg of carbon dioxide. Global greenhouse gas emissions measured in carbon dioxide equivalents consist of 74.4 per cent carbon dioxide and 17.3 per cent methane,[6] making them the two most important greenhouse gases to tackle. Across a shorter time horizon of twenty years, methane has an even higher GWP of 81.2,[7] making it particularly impactful on warming in the near future. Methane is thus a crucial factor in this decade's challenge of achieving immediate and drastic reductions in greenhouse gas emissions.

SOURCES OF METHANE COME FROM VARIOUS SECTORS

Around 60 per cent of global methane emissions are human-caused, and this comes largely from agriculture, fossil fuels and waste.[8] Agricultural

---

[4] International Energy Agency (IEA), "Global Methane Tracker 2022 – Analysis", https://www.iea.org/reports/global-methane-tracker-2022 (accessed 10 March 2022).

[5] Valérie Masson-Delmotte et al., "IPCC, 2021: Summary for Policymakers", in *Climate Change 2021: The Physical Science Basis*, Contribution of Working Group I to the Sixth Assessment Report of the Intergovernmental Panel on Climate Change" (Cambridge University Press, 2021).

[6] Ritchie and Roser, "CO_2 and Greenhouse Gas Emissions".

[7] C. Smith et al., "The Earth's Energy Budget, Climate Feedbacks, and Climate Sensitivity Supplementary Material", in *Climate Change 2021: The Physical Science Basis.* Contribution of Working Group I to the Sixth Assessment Report of the Intergovernmental Panel on Climate Change [V. Masson-Delmotte, P. Zhai, A. Pirani, S.L. Connors, C. Péan, S. Berger, N. Caud, Y. Chen, L. Goldfarb, M.I. Gomis, M. Huang, K. Leitzell, E. Lonnoy, J.B.R. Matthews, T.K. Maycock, T. Waterfield, O. Yelekçi, R. Yu, and B. Zhou, eds.]", n.d., https://www.ipcc.ch/

[8] United Nations Environment Programme (UNEP) and Climate and Clean Air Coalition (CCAC), "Global Methane Assessment: Benefits and Costs of Mitigating Methane Emissions" (Nairobi: United Nations Environment Programme, 2021).

emissions are mainly attributed to enteric fermentation (digestive processes in animals like cattle) and manure in livestock as well as rice cultivation, where methane-emitting bacteria grow in flooded rice paddies.[9] In this article, estimates of animal agricultural production exclude eggs, the production of which does not have significant methane emissions.[10] Within fossil fuels, oil, gas and coal all contribute significantly. Oil and gas operations involve both intentional and unintentional methane emissions. Unintentional emissions, known as "fugitive emissions", occur from leaks in infrastructure that allow natural gas (mainly consisting of methane) to escape. Intentional emissions are caused by routine burning (known as "flaring") or release (known as "venting") to dispose of natural gas that is not financially viable to store. Venting results in greater emissions than flaring. Certain equipment such as motors and pumps with inefficient designs also produce methane emissions during regular operations.[11] In the coal sector, methane emissions are generated from leakages in mines.[12]

GLOBAL AND REGIONAL ACTION ON METHANE SO FAR

Global efforts to target methane emissions, especially in the fossil fuel sector, have grown steadily over the years. The Climate and Clean Air Coalition (CCAC) is a global network of state and non-state actors formed by the UN Environment Programme (UNEP) and several governments in 2012 to target short-lived climate pollutants. Its work includes the CCAC Oil and Gas Methane Partnership (OGMP) (started in 2015), an

---

[9] Ibid.

[10] Rocío Abín et al., "Environmental Assesment of Intensive Egg Production: A Spanish Case Study", *Journal of Cleaner Production* 179 (April 2018): 160–68, https://doi.org/10.1016/j.jclepro.2018.01.067

[11] International Energy Agency (IEA), "Methane Emissions from Oil and Gas – Analysis", November 2021, https://www.iea.org/reports/methane-emissions-from-oil-and-gas

[12] IEA, "Global Methane Tracker 2022 – Analysis".

initiative to reduce methane emissions in the oil and gas sector. Together with oil and gas companies and other partners, the CCAC launched an updated framework for methane reporting called the OGMP 2.0 in 2020 to encourage wider participation and credibility in climate mitigation efforts. It also contributed in 2021 to the Global Methane Assessment, a comprehensive report on methane emissions reduction potential, which found that anthropogenic methane can be reduced by up to 45 per cent in this decade.[13] In 2022–24, a new partnership called the CCAC Methane Flagship will engage and mobilize partners through scientific expertise, decision-making tools and political engagement, including the scale-up of financing to help build an enabling environment for methane emissions reductions aligned with the Global Methane Assessment.

The Global Methane Initiative (GMI), launched in 2004, is a public-private collaboration on methane reduction projects, in which Indonesia, the Philippines, Thailand and Vietnam are already partners. The GMI has sponsored and participated in events such as the Asia Pacific Global Methane Initiative Oil and Gas Sector Workshops held in Jakarta in 2011 and 2012, wherein government and private sector representatives discussed best practices in methane reduction measures.[14]

At present, global ambition on methane is greater than ever—sadly, many initiatives have emerged only in recent years even though scientists have been aware of methane's impact since the 1990s. Be that as it may, in this region, activities targeting methane abatement remain relatively scarce. With a few exceptions, almost all GMI activities held in ASEAN partner countries occurred within the last decade. While the OGMP 2.0 framework aims to harmonize reporting and improve credibility globally, most of its private sector members are based in Europe and only one is

---

[13] UNEP and CCAC, "Global Methane Assessment: Benefits and Costs of Mitigating Methane Emissions".

[14] Global Methane Initiative (GMI), "1st Asia Pacific Global Methane Initiative Oil and Gas Sector Workshop", https://www.globalmethane.org/events/details.aspx?eventid=353 (accessed 10 March 2022); "2nd Asia Pacific Global Methane Initiative Oil and Gas Sector Workshop", https://www.globalmethane.org/events/details.aspx?eventid=396 (accessed 10 March 2022).

based in ASEAN, i.e., PTT Exploration and Production Public Company Limited (PPTEP), a Thai national petroleum company.[15] Nevertheless, this could change given the participation of several ASEAN countries in the Global Methane Pledge, another initiative that sparked active discourse on methane in the region in the weeks after its announcement and raised awareness of the importance of methane emissions.

Formally announced at COP26, the Global Methane Pledge is a commitment by over 100 countries to cut global methane emissions by at least 30 per cent from 2020 levels by 2030—a slightly lower number than what is required for a 1.5 degrees scenario. The participating countries account for almost half of global anthropogenic methane emissions. The Pledge is one of the few recent developments on methane that has had significant participation from the Southeast Asian region. Five ASEAN countries have joined the Pledge: Indonesia, Malaysia, the Philippines, Singapore and Vietnam. Their combined methane emissions in 2018 amounted to around 6.5 per cent of the global total,[16] with Indonesia alone accounting for 4.0 per cent as the seventh-largest emitter. Malaysia, the Philippines and Vietnam ranked in the top twenty-five country emitters, along with Thailand and Myanmar which were not part of the Pledge. Regional media highlighted that Indonesia's participation was significant, while other major emitters like China, India and Russia were absent from the pledge. Globally, attention was brought to the oil and gas sector and the agriculture sector for action on methane. Many pointed out that while the oil and gas industry is the low-hanging fruit due to its considerable potential for cheap methane abatement solutions, both oil and coal usage are continuing to grow rapidly in Asia and Southeast Asia. Researchers from the International Rice Research Institute have

---

[15] Oil and Gas Methane Partnership 2.0 and United Nations Environment Programme and Climate, "List of OGMP 2.0 Member Companies", January 2022, https://www.ogmpartnership.com/sites/default/files/files/List-of-OGMP-2.0-member-companies_15-02-22.pdf

[16] World Resources Institute (WRI), "Climate Watch Historical GHG Emissions", 2021, https://www.climatewatchdata.org/ghg-emissions

argued for greater investment in improved rice cultivation practices and irrigation infrastructure, emphasizing that employing new techniques in Vietnam's Mekong River Delta region alone could reduce 5.6 MtCO2e in emissions annually.[17] At the COP26 launch of the Pledge, Vietnam's Prime Minister Pham Minh Chinh also called on developed countries to share support through investments as well as capacity-building to help developed countries reduce methane emissions.[18] This big shift in regional attention and ambition on methane is an encouraging trend that calls for stronger sector-based implementation of methane emissions reduction solutions.

SECTORS FOR METHANE ABATEMENT: OIL AND GAS, COAL AND WASTE

The Global Methane Assessment 2021[19] synthesized findings on the estimated cost and abatement potential of various methane abatement solutions across sectors and regions. It was found that low-cost abatement in oil and gas (only solutions costing US$600/t of methane or US$21/tCO2e and below) have abatement potentials ranging from 18 to 32 Mt/year. When oil and gas solutions at all costs are considered, the maximum abatement potential increases to 29–57 Mt/year. Low-cost abatement in the waste sector ranges from 10 to 20 Mt/year. In the agriculture sector, low-cost solutions are fewer and uncertainties are greater: livestock measures are estimated to cost US$600/t or US$1,000/t, with abatement potentials ranging anywhere between 4 and 42 Mt/year; rice cultivation measures vary greatly from US$150 to US$3,000/t with an abatement potential of 6–9 Mt/year.

---

[17] Oliver Frith, Reiner Wassmann, and Bjoern Ole Sander. "How Asia's Rice Producers Can Help Limit Global Warming", *The Diplomat*, 13 October 2021, https://thediplomat.com/2021/10/how-asias-rice-producers-can-help-limit-global-warming/

[18] *The Voice of Vietnam*, "Vietnam Joins Global Pledge to Reduce Methane Emissions, Reverse Deforestation", 3 November 2021, https://vovworld.vn/en-US/content/OTAxNDgy.vov

[19] UNEP and CCAC, "Global Methane Assessment: Benefits and Costs of Mitigating Methane Emissions".

Based on abatement measures with negative net costs, the greatest potential for economic benefits is in the oil and gas sector, and in the waste sector. In the Asia-Pacific region, the largest abatement potentials (considering measures at all costs) are in the coal sector and waste sector. Abatement measures in the coal sector include technical adjustments like pre-mining degasification (which captures methane) and the flooding of abandoned coal mines, as well as long-term behavioural and technological changes like switching to renewable energy and carbon pricing.[20] In 2020, coal accounted for 31.4 per cent of ASEAN's installed power capacity, which amounts to almost 90 GW. Since then, it has continued to grow at a rapid pace, with 22 GW of capacity added in 2020 alone.[21] Introducing methane abatement solutions to existing coal mines while working to replace coal power with renewables would influence a significant amount of current and future methane emissions from coal. This would also align ASEAN countries with the Glasgow Climate Pact's commitment to "phasedown" unabated coal power.

Low and negative-cost solutions are also abundant in the Asia-Pacific region's oil and gas sector, especially in leak detection and repair (LDAR), which has great negative costs and high abatement potential across both oil and gas (see Annex 1). Other measures which have high abatement potential and negative or low costs include blowdown capture (the recovery of excess gas that is otherwise vented or flared when equipment is routinely depressurized) and the replacement of equipment parts.

PROPORTIONAL REGIONAL CONTRIBUTIONS BY SECTOR CONSISTENT OVER TIME

ASEAN countries' combined methane emissions amounted to 736 MtCO2e (including land-use change and forestry, or LUCF) and 680.3 MtCO2e (excluding LUCF) in 2018. When excluding emissions

---

[20] United Nations Environment Programme and Climate and Clean Air Coalition.

[21] ASEAN Centre for Energy, "ASEAN Power Updates 2021", September 2021, https://aseanenergy.org/asean-power-updates-2021/

from LUCF (which fluctuates widely), the region's total methane emissions have grown steadily since 1990, mostly due to emissions growth in the agriculture sector, which is the largest contributor. In 2018, agriculture accounted for 354.2 MtCO2e of methane emissions, while waste accounted for 201.4 MtCO2e. Although such sector proportions have remained rather consistent at the regional level, they vary considerably at the country level. See Figure 1.

SECTOR CONTRIBUTIONS OF INDIVIDUAL COUNTRIES VARY WIDELY

As described earlier, methane emissions can come from multiple sectors, especially the fossil fuel, agriculture and waste sectors. Given that ASEAN is a diverse group of countries with widely varying sizes and economic activities, their contributions to methane emissions, and by extension their optimal methane reduction strategies, also differ. The following section briefly summarizes the main sources of methane emissions from each ASEAN country.

Brunei

The overwhelming majority of Brunei's methane emissions is from fugitive emissions (consistently over 97 per cent), which consists of methane emitted from oil and gas systems and coal mining.[22] As much as 9 kt, or 26.8 per cent of the total methane emissions from the oil and gas sector in 2020, were fugitive emissions.[23] *Oil and gas producers in Brunei thus have significant potential for low-cost methane mitigation.*

Cambodia

Cambodia's methane emissions are dominated by the agriculture sector, which accounted for an annual average of 78.1 per cent of emissions in

---

[22] WRI, "Climate Watch Historical GHG Emissions".

[23] IEA, "Global Methane Tracker 2022 – Analysis".

Figure 1: Methane Emissions in ASEAN by Sector

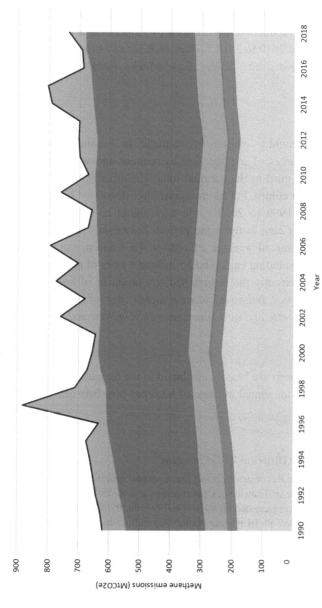

Note: Data are unavailable for the Transport and Manufacturing sectors.
Source: World Resources Institute, "Climate Watch Historical GHG Emissions", 2021, https://www.climatewatchdata.org/ghg-emissions

2010–18[24] and is steadily growing in impact. Its growth in agriculture production is partly attributed to expansion in paddy rice production;[25] while meat and milk production has declined by 12 per cent and 10 per cent respectively from 2010 to 2018.[26] *Thus, tackling its rice production subsector would drastically lower Cambodia's overall methane emissions.*

Indonesia

Being the largest country emitter of methane in Southeast Asia, Indonesia's main sources of methane are agriculture and waste; both contribute roughly a third to the national total. Historically, waste has been the much bigger culprit, but its emissions have decreased by about 16.3 per cent from 1990 to 2018 while agricultural emissions have increased by 47.2 per cent in the same period. Indonesia's agriculture sector produced an annual average of almost 4.5 million tonnes of livestock products (excluding eggs) and 55 million tonnes of paddy rice in 2000–20.[27] It is currently the largest ASEAN producer of both rice and livestock products.[28] *Indonesia faces the challenge of addressing methane in both the waste and agriculture sectors simultaneously.*

Laos

Laos' methane emissions are heavily attributed to the agriculture sector, which accounted for an annual average of 83.6 per cent between 2010

---

[24] WRI, "Climate Watch Historical GHG Emissions".

[25] International Bank for Reconstruction and Development and the World Bank, "Cambodian Agriculture in Transition: Opportunities and Risks", 2015, https://documents1.worldbank.org/curated/en/805091467993504209/pdf/96308-ESW-KH-White-cover-P145838-PUBLIC-Cambodian-Agriculture-in-Transition.pdf

[26] Hannah Ritchie and Max Roser, "Meat and Dairy Production", *Our World in Data*, 25 August 2017, https://ourworldindata.org/meat-production

[27] Food and Agriculture Organization (FAO), "Crops and Livestock Products", https://www.fao.org/faostat/en/#data/QCL/ (accessed 18 February 2022).

[28] Ibid.

and 2018.[29] Paddy rice is Laos' most-produced agricultural commodity; meat production, while less significant in volume, increased by 20 per cent from 2010 to 2018.[30] *Laos' main focus for methane is the agriculture sector, which is dominated by rice production.*

Malaysia

Malaysia's largest sources of methane are waste and fugitive emissions, which accounted for 39.3 per cent and 40.5 per cent of methane emissions as annual averages respectively from 2010 to 2018.[31] Its oil and gas sector alone produced 404.4 kt of methane emissions in 2020, of which 28.6 per cent were fugitive emissions.[32] *Malaysia's biggest opportunities for tackling methane emissions lie in the oil and gas sector.*

Myanmar

The largest methane contributor in Myanmar is by far the agriculture sector, which accounted for 82.1 per cent of countrywide methane emissions on average in 2010–18.[33] Paddy rice is Myanmar's top agricultural commodity by production quantity. Though rice production went through a decline from 2009 to 2016, production picked up from 2016 and reached over 27 million tonnes in 2018.[34] In addition, Myanmar produced an annual average of over 4.5 million tonnes of livestock products (excluding eggs).[35] *Efforts on methane reduction should be focused on both rice and livestock (especially dairy) in the agriculture sector.*

---

[29] WRI, "Climate Watch Historical GHG Emissions".

[30] FAO, "Crops and Livestock Products".

[31] WRI, "Climate Watch Historical GHG Emissions".

[32] IEA, "Global Methane Tracker 2022 – Analysis".

[33] WRI, "Climate Watch Historical GHG Emissions".

[34] FAO, "Crops and Livestock Products".

[35] Ibid.

The Philippines

The Philippines' largest methane emitting sector is agriculture, but a significant proportion is also attributed to waste. Agriculture contributed 75.6 per cent of methane emissions on average annually between 2010 and 2018, while waste contributed 17.3 per cent on average.[36] Paddy rice is the second-largest agricultural commodity by production quantity (after sugar cane). It increased significantly in volume by 20.9 per cent from 2010 to 2018.[37] Meat production also increased by 25 per cent from 2010 to 2018,[38] with a relatively greater proportion of pork production than in other ASEAN countries. Livestock production, in general, has been rising steadily, peaking at over 25 million tonnes in 2017.[39] *The Philippines should tackle both rice and livestock (including manure management in pork production) in its agriculture sector.*

Thailand

Thailand's key sector for methane is agriculture, which contributes 60.7 per cent to the national total in 2018. This is no surprise given that Thailand, along with Indonesia, is one of the world's top producers of rice.[40] While its livestock production quantity fluctuates across time, its annual average has been substantial at 3.7 million tonnes over the past two decades.[41] Nevertheless, contributions from fugitive emissions and waste have also gained ground since the mid-1990s and are worthy of attention. *Thailand's main challenge for methane reduction is in rice production due to its large contribution, but it can also take advantage of opportunities in the oil and gas sector.*

---

[36] WRI, "Climate Watch Historical GHG Emissions".

[37] FAO, "Crops and Livestock Products".

[38] Ibid.

[39] Ibid.

[40] Ibid.

[41] Ibid.

Singapore

Singapore's largest contributor of methane is from the waste sector, followed by methane from fugitive emissions. Waste has consistently dominated Singapore's methane emissions profile and has more than doubled from 2000 to 2018. Fugitive emissions have also grown by 83.0 per cent in the same period. *Efforts to reduce methane should be taken in both the waste and oil and gas sectors.*

Vietnam

Vietnam's largest methane contributor is the agriculture sector, which made up 56.3 per cent of total methane emissions on average in 2010–18. Paddy rice is Vietnam's most produced agricultural commodity.[42] While meat and milk production are less prominent, they grew considerably in 2010–18 by 31 per cent and 185 per cent respectively. The waste sector, which contributed 16.2 per cent on average, is also a significant source. *Vietnam can make use of opportunities to reduce methane emissions in the waste and oil and gas sectors, but its main contributor to emissions is agriculture (mainly rice).*

STANDOUT TRENDS IN COUNTRY-LEVEL EMISSIONS

Government planners and business corporations will need to watch out for three trends in the near future. Methane emissions from the agriculture sector in Indonesia rose from 82.6 Mt in 2003 to 100.5 Mt in 2012 (Figure 2). The average annual increase was 2 Mt in this period; with an accelerated average annual increase of 4 Mt in 2013–17 This accelerated increase is a significant contrast to the long-term plateau between 1995 and 2002 and is coarsely correlated with the huge growth in GDP per capita in the country. However, the rise in methane emissions

---

[42] Ibid.

Figure 2: Methane Emissions from the Agriculture Sector of Indonesia, Myanmar, Philippines, Thailand and Vietnam

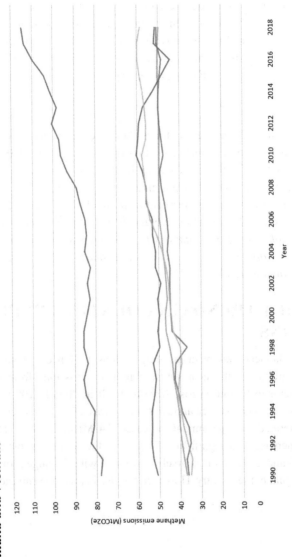

Source: World Resources Institute, "Climate Watch Historical GHG Emissions", 2021, https://www.climatewatchdata.org/ghg-emissions

may not be attributable to domestic food consumption. The rice and maize consumption of the Indonesians had started levelling off before the country went through an economic boom.[43] The export of food products, however, has been going up since 2003, primarily to the United States, the Netherlands, Singapore and Japan.[44]

Agricultural methane emissions in Thailand could not be more different from that of Indonesia, and have fluctuated within the narrow range of 49 to 54 Mt from 1990 to 2006 (Figure 2). From 2007 till 2013, emissions rose before diving from their lowest point of 44 Mt in 2016 as the Thai economy slowed down. Analysts have pointed out that the lower-than-expected economic growth was a result of reduced exports to the slowed-down Chinese market. The economic challenges coincided with the political uncertainty that came in the wake of the 2014 election in Thailand.[45] Having said that, the export of food products to China and Indonesia in that period were not as severely affected as that to the United States and Japan.[46] On the other hand, Thailand as the largest rubber producer in the world exported significantly less rubber to China during that period of economic downturn. Rubber plantation and

[43] Bustanul Arifin et al., "Modeling the Future of Indonesian Food Consumption: Final Report", *World Food Programme*, Jakarta, June 2018, p. 69.

[44] World Integrated Trade Solution, "Indonesia Food Products Exports by Country US$000 1989–2019 | WITS Data", https://wits.worldbank.org/CountryProfile/en/Country/IDN/StartYear/1989/EndYear/2019/TradeFlow/Export/Indicator/XPRT-TRD-VL/Partner/BY-COUNTRY/Product/16-24_FoodProd (accessed 11 March 2022).

[45] Edward Barbour-Lacey, "Thailand Economic Growth to Be Curtailed in 2015, 2016 to Be Brighter", *ASEAN Briefing*, 26 June 2015, https://www.aseanbriefing.com/news/thailand-economic-growth-to-be-curtailed-in-2015-2016-to-be-brighter/

[46] World Integrated Trade Solution, "Thailand Food Products Exports by Country US$000 1988–2019 | WITS Data", https://wits.worldbank.org/CountryProfile/en/Country/THA/StartYear/1988/EndYear/2019/TradeFlow/Export/Indicator/XPRT-TRD-VL/Partner/BY-COUNTRY/Product/16-24_FoodProd (accessed 11 March 2022).

production emits methane mainly during the use of energy and synthetic fertilizer.[47]

In the past thirty years, Myanmar's methane emission has been on an upward trajectory and this growth rate is at least parallel to that of Indonesia's. It saw a 71 per cent increase compared to Indonesia's 47 per cent for the same period. However, Myanmar's emissions levelled off between 2015 and 2018 (Figure 2). This "boom and plateau" trend seems to correspond well with the country's economic activity. The steady rise in GDP per capita between 1992 and 2006 may not surprise most analysts, but the next seven years saw an exponential growth that the agriculture-dependent country had not seen before, contributing to the slight rise in agricultural methane emissions. The levelling off of emissions could partially be explained by the hesitancy of investors to pour money into the country in the absence of more progressive economic reforms.[48] Myanmar has been a large exporter of rice to China for the past decade.[49] However, rice export amounts have fallen short of the government's target due to strong competition from neighbouring countries and the poor quality of its rice products. On top of these factors is the worrisome problem of irrigation in Myanmar hampering the total yield.[50] While this may drive down the overall methane emissions of the

---

[47] Warit Jawjit, Carolien Kroeze, and Suwat Rattanapan, "Greenhouse Gas Emissions from Rubber Industry in Thailand", *Journal of Cleaner Production* 18, no. 5 (March 2010): 403–11, https://doi.org/10.1016/j.jclepro.2009.12.003

[48] Kristian Stokke, Roman Vakulchuk, and Indra Øverland, "Myanmar: A Political Economy Analysis", Norwegian Institute of International Affairs, 2018, p. 98.

[49] World Bank, "Myanmar: Capitalizing on Rice Export Opportunities", 2014, https://documents.worldbank.org/en/publication/documents-reports/documentdetail/570771468323340471/myanmar-capitalizing-on-rice-export-opportunities

[50] International Trade Administration, U.S. Department of Commerce, "Burma – Agriculture", 27 September 2021, https://www.trade.gov/country-commercial-guides/burma-agriculture

country, this incident calls for a comprehensive evaluation of the rice species used and of the agricultural practices. Improvement of any of these will significantly reduce the methane footprint of Myanmar, which is likely to keep its rice bowl status.

The three trends above show that we need to pay more attention to the methane emissions of fast-growing countries that depend on agricultural products. These observed correlations between patterns of economic metrics and methane emissions indicate that ASEAN's methane emissions can be expected to continue rising as its overall economy grows. As with carbon dioxide, methane emissions should be decoupled as much as possible from economic activity. This is especially true for large producers of rice. More alarming is that these products are not eventually consumed by domestic residents, and are primarily exported to wealthy countries. This calls for greater responsibility on the part of importing countries to help with methane-abating agricultural practices in the export countries.

COLLABORATION AT THE SUBREGIONAL LEVEL

ASEAN countries differ greatly in their methane emissions, both in magnitude and in sector contributions. At the same time, methane abatement itself is a complicated area spanning several distinct sectors, each with a different set of challenges, solutions and levels of affordability. While rice cultivation is the primary source of methane emissions in Southeast Asia, not all countries face the same sets of challenges. Moreover, fugitive emissions from the oil and gas sector are easier to abate, and their makeup in the overall emissions profile is much more significant in some countries. Methane emissions from waste management are at the same time an under-acknowledged area. Therefore, Southeast Asian countries can be grouped in the following three categories to inform national-level prioritization. While it may be difficult to coordinate any overarching regional planning or initiatives on methane, those with common methane focus areas can still work together to jointly tackle the challenges of methane abatement specific to them.

Focus Group 1: Agriculture

The first group consists of countries that have more than half of their methane emissions coming from the agriculture sector (Figure 3). When it comes to agricultural methane, the global spotlight is often on livestock; but for the ASEAN region in particular, methane emissions from rice cultivation are also of considerable if not of greater concern. In 2020, the seven ASEAN countries in this group produced around 2.1 per cent of the global total of livestock products (excluding eggs) and 19.2 per cent of the global total of paddy rice.[51] This is no surprise, especially for large rice producers such as Myanmar, Thailand, Vietnam, the Philippines and Indonesia.[52]

While Cambodia and Laos have not been featured as the rice bowls of the world, their methane emissions from the agricultural sector took up around one-fifth of their total national emissions. It is worth examining if the inefficient agricultural practice is one of the drivers.

As mentioned earlier, Thailand relies on rubber exports in addition to being a major rice producer, which may also be a factor in its methane emissions, given the sheer amount of rubber produced in the country— over 4.8 million tonnes in 2019.[53]

Cambodia, Indonesia, Myanmar, Thailand and Vietnam have already been involved in projects under the Sustainable Rice Platform, which claims to help cut greenhouse gas emissions (including methane) in addition to raising incomes and cutting water consumption (Sustainable Rice Platform, 2020).[54] Although Myanmar has not included methane in its NDC greenhouse gas coverage (the only ASEAN country yet to do so), it has recognized that the waste management interventions proposed in its NDC adaptation strategy can include methane abatement to achieve

---

[51] FAO, "Crops and Livestock Products".

[52] Ibid.

[53] Ibid.

[54] Sustainable Rice Platform, "Annual Report 2020", 2020, https://www.sustainablerice.org/wp-content/uploads/2022/01/SRP-Annual-Report-2020.pdf

Figure 3: Methane Emissions by Sector of Cambodia, Indonesia, Laos, Myanmar, the Philippines, Thailand and Vietnam in 2018

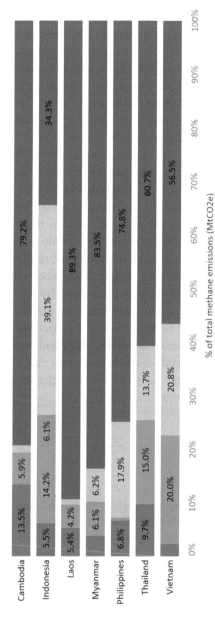

Source: World Resources Institute, "Climate Watch Historical GHG Emissions", 2021, https://www.climatewatchdata.org/ghg-emissions

mitigation co-benefits. Myanmar also plans to take up capacity-building activities in climate-smart agriculture to build agricultural resilience. This strategy may help Myanmar tackle methane emissions while maintaining competitiveness as a rice exporter. Depending on the type of climate-smart agriculture practices implemented, this could also contribute to methane abatement. Similarly, Laos' adaptation strategy includes the improvement of water practices in rice cultivation, while Cambodia's NDC adaptation strategy includes capacity building for increased climate resilience in rice cultivation, and identifies mitigation as one of the co-benefits.

In the Philippines, Alternate Wetting and Drying techniques have been extensively studied since the early 2000s due to their effectiveness in reducing greenhouse gas emissions and boosting climate resilience. But despite efforts at scaling up, adoption was seen to be limited to less than 5 per cent of the total irrigated area nationwide in 2016 due to constraints in institutional enforcement, incentives and regulations.[55]

The challenge of methane abatement in agriculture, especially in rice cultivation which is a major contributor to these countries' economies, is evident from the relatively high estimated costs and limited success notwithstanding past efforts. While this group of countries has already started to explore low-carbon transitions in agriculture and may benefit from the sharing of experiences and lessons learned, they may also need greater support beyond technology transfer, to design effective policies for the scaling up of abatement measures.

---

[55] Yuji Enriquez et al., "Disentangling Challenges to Scaling Alternate Wetting and Drying Technology for Rice Cultivation: Distilling Lessons From 20 Years of Experience in the Philippines", *Frontiers in Sustainable Food Systems* 5 (2021), https://www.frontiersin.org/article/10.3389/fsufs.2021.675818; Vladislav Arnaoudov, Evangeline B. Sibayan and Raymond C. Caguioa, "Adaptation and Mitigation Initiatives in Philippine Rice Cultivation" (United Nations Development Programme, 2015), https://www.undp.org/sites/g/files/zskgke326/files/publications/AMIA Philippines Final.pdf

Focus Group 2: Waste

As mentioned before, Indonesia has an issue with waste-induced methane emissions. But so do Malaysia and Singapore, both of which are not agricultural nations (Figure 4). Three-quarters of Singapore's methane emission comes from waste, while Malaysia emits almost as much methane in the waste sector as in the oil and gas sector. These three countries may benefit from greater collaboration in waste management, given their geographical proximity and historical ties to each other. The changes over time have been fairly dramatic. In the first twelve years of this century, Indonesia halved its waste-induced methane emissions while emissions in Malaysia increased by more than half and continued to grow till at least 2018 (Figure 5). Singapore's emissions from the waste sector have been growing steadily from 1990 to 2005 at an annual rate of 49 per cent. After that, the annual increase became much steeper, rising at a rate of 82 per cent.[56]

Indonesia's NDC includes plans for methane abatement in both landfills and wastewater treatment. The Singapore Green Plan 2030 has targets to reduce the amount of waste to landfill per capita per day by 20 per cent by 2026, and 30 per cent by 2030. While Singapore does not have a target for wastewater treatment, it has installed a new plant for wastewater sludge incineration that reduces emissions by 129 ktCO2e per year and generates carbon credits.[57] Similarly, Clean Development Mechanism waste-to-energy projects in Malaysia have involved the installation of biogas recovery systems for palm oil waste effluent, which generate emissions reductions.[58] Malaysia also has several existing and

---

[56] WRI, "Climate Watch Historical GHG Emissions".

[57] National Climate Change Secretariat Singapore, "Waste And Water", https://www.nccs.gov.sg/singapores-climate-action/waste-and-water/ (accessed 11 March 2022).

[58] Clean Development Mechanism, "CDM: Methane Recovery and Utilisation Project at TSH Lahad Datu Palm Oil Mill, Sabah, Malaysia", 2012, https://cdm.unfccc.int/Projects/DB/DNV-CUK1227799476.62/view; Clean Development Mechanism, "CDM: Methane Recovery and Utilisation Project at TSH Sabahan Palm Oil Mill, Sabah, Malaysia", 2012, https://cdm.unfccc.int/Projects/DB/DNV-CUK1227800277.92/view

Figure 4: Methane Emissions by Sector of Indonesia, Malaysia and Singapore in 2018

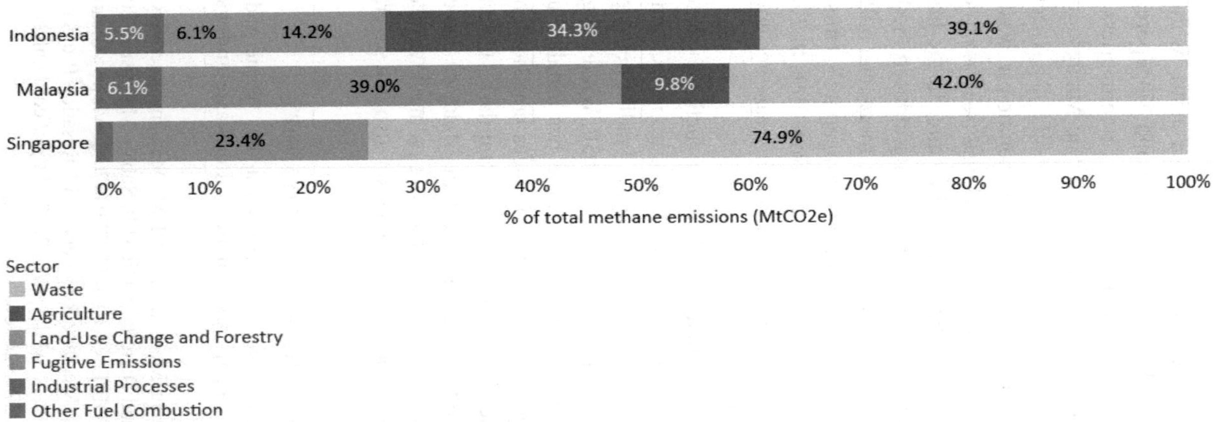
Indonesia
5.5%
6.1%
14.2%
34.3%
39.1%
Malaysia
6.1%
39.0%
9.8%
42.0%
Singapore
23.4%
74.9%
0%
10%
20%
30%
40%
50%
60%
70%
80%
90%
100%
% of total methane emissions (MtCO2e)
Sector
Waste
Agriculture
Land-Use Change and Forestry
Fugitive Emissions
Industrial Processes
Other Fuel Combustion

Source: World Resources Institute, "Climate Watch Historical GHG Emissions", 2021, https://www.climatewatchdata.org/ghg-emissions

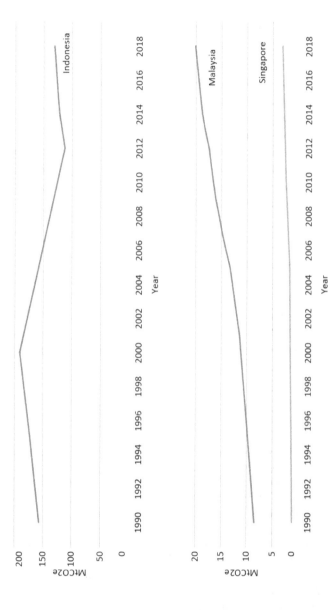

Figure 5: Methane Emissions from the Waste Sector of Indonesia, Malaysia and Singapore in 1990–2018

Source: World Resources Institute, "Climate Watch Historical GHG Emissions", 2021, https://www.climatewatchdata.org/ghg-emissions

upcoming waste-to-energy projects, known as landfill biogas plants, that involve the capture of methane gas from landfills for electricity production,[59] while Singapore already relies greatly on waste-to-energy plants for its solid waste management.[60] A study of landfill gas power plant projects in Indonesia found that their limited success was due to obstacles such as financial support, regulatory barriers and insufficient awareness among communities and government institutions.[61]

All three countries face the challenge of mitigating emissions from landfills and wastewater while reducing waste production and have already made different levels of progress in implementing methane abatement measures. This puts them in a good position for collaboration on technical issues like the management of incineration residue and toxic emissions, as well as the eventual scaling up of such measures.

Focus Group 3: Oil and Gas

It is unsurprising that Brunei and Malaysia—the two nations highly dependent on oil and gas exports—have such a significant proportion of their methane emissions coming from that industry.

Brunei's methane emissions are heavily dominated by fossil fuels, while over a third of Malaysia's methane emissions can be attributed to these (Figure 6). Given that abatement in the oil and gas sector has the

---

[59] Zi Jun Yong et al., "Sustainable Waste-to-Energy Development in Malaysia: Appraisal of Environmental, Financial, and Public Issues Related with Energy Recovery from Municipal Solid Waste", *Processes* 7, no. 10 (October 2019): 676, https://doi.org/10.3390/pr7100676

[60] National Environment Agency Singapore, "Solid Waste Management Infrastructure", https://www.nea.gov.sg/our-services/waste-management/3r-programmes-and-resources/waste-management-infrastructure/solid-waste-management-infrastructure (accessed 11 March 2022).

[61] R. Budiarto et al., "Sustainability Challenges of the Landfill Gas Power Plants in Indonesia", *IOP Conference Series: Earth and Environmental Science* 940, no. 1 (December 2021): 012028, https://doi.org/10.1088/1755-1315/940/1/012028

Figure 6: Methane Emissions by Sector of Brunei and Malaysia in 2018

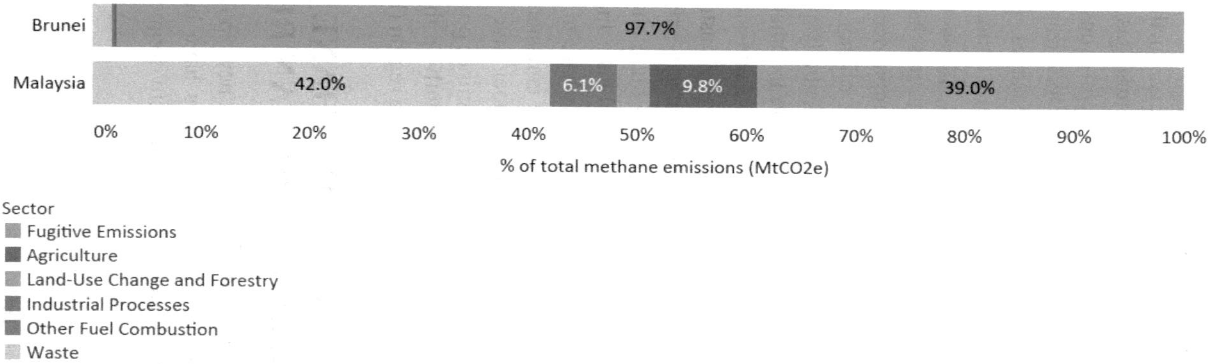

Brunei
97.7%
Malaysia
42.0%
6.1%
9.8%
39.0%
0%
10%
20%
30%
40%
50%
60%
70%
80%
90%
100%
% of total methane emissions (MtCO2e)
Sector
Fugitive Emissions
Agriculture
Land-Use Change and Forestry
Industrial Processes
Other Fuel Combustion
Waste

Source: World Resources Institute, "Climate Watch Historical GHG Emissions", 2021, https://www.climatewatchdata.org/ghg-emissions

most economic benefits, this puts them in a favourable position to set high ambitions for methane abatement.

In both countries, the majority of oil and gas methane emissions are from the intentional venting or flaring of natural gas, but a fair portion (over 20 per cent) are unintentional fugitive emissions (Figure 7).

Many abatement measures help capture monetizable natural gas that would have otherwise been lost through leakages, venting or flaring. Table 1 shows the three cheapest abatement options for Brunei and Malaysia's oil and gas sectors. These include options with high negative net costs. For both countries, all three measures have negative costs across oil and gas operations. For instance, implementing upstream leak detection and repair (LDAR) in Malaysia's offshore gas sector could result in gains of US$30.59/MBtu and potentially prevent 50.7 kt of methane emissions (or 1,413.1 ktCO2e) per year. Other measures include installing vapour recovery units that capture emissions and replacing conventional pumps (which vent natural gas) with instrument air systems that perform the same functions without causing venting.[62]

However, it would be misleading not to highlight the large oil and gas producers in the region. By sheer volume, Indonesia, Thailand and Vietnam have contributed a significant share to the regional total (Figure 8). In the past twenty years, methane emissions from the oil and gas industry in Indonesia, Malaysia and Brunei have been fairly stable. While Thailand and Vietnam were relatively minor producers in the early 1990s, both increased their activity significantly in the early 2000s and have become notable energy producers in the region (Figure 8).

ASEAN ACTIONS ON METHANE ARE PROMISING, BUT MORE CAN BE DONE

Though the Global Methane Pledge shone a new spotlight on methane, actions to deal with the problems it causes have been underway for several years in Southeast Asia. Many environmental and climate

---

[62] IEA, "Global Methane Tracker 2022 – Analysis".

Figure 7: Oil and Gas Methane Emissions of Brunei and Malaysia in 2020

Reason
- Incomplete-flare
- Fugitive
- Vented

Brunei: 66.1% | 26.9% | 7.0%

Malaysia: 59.6% | 28.6% | 11.7%

Source: International Energy Agency (IEA), "Methane Tracker 2021 – Analysis", https://www.iea.org/reports/methane-tracker-2021 (accessed 11 March 2022).

Table 1: Cheapest Abatement Options for Brunei and Malaysia's Oil and Gas Sector

Brunei						
Type of Abatement Measure		Downstream Gas	Offshore Gas	Offshore Oil	Onshore Conventional Gas	Onshore Conventional Oil
Upstream LDAR	Savings (kt)		5.93	1.11	0.34	0.08
	Cost (US$/MBtu)		–30.59	–30.59	–32.70	–32.70
Vapour recovery units	Savings (kt)	0.01	1.63	4.85	0.01	0.40
	Cost (US$/MBtu)	–2.46	–7.08	–15.17	–2.46	–10.65
Replace pumps with instrument air systems	Savings (kt)	0.02	0.74	0.81	0.20	0.19
	Cost (US$/MBtu)	–9.25	–9.25	–9.25	–6.73	–6.73

Malaysia						
Type of Abatement Measure		Downstream Gas	Downstream Oil	Offshore Gas	Offshore Oil	Onshore Conventional Oil
Upstream LDAR	Savings (kt)			50.65	8.55	0.11
	Cost (US$/MBtu)			–30.59	–30.59	–32.70
Vapour recovery units	Savings (kt)	0.12	0.06	13.95	51.03	5.28
	Cost (US$/MBtu)	–3.52	–3.52	–7.46	–15.78	–11.93
Replace pumps with instrument air systems	Savings (kt)	0.24		6.32	6.24	0.26
	Cost (US$/MBtu)	–9.25		–9.25	–9.25	–6.73

Source: International Energy Agency (IEA), "Methane Tracker 2021 – Analysis", https://www.iea.org/reports/methane-tracker-2021 (accessed 11 March 2022).

28

Figure 8: Top 5 Producers of Fugitive Methane Emissions in the Oil and Gas Sector

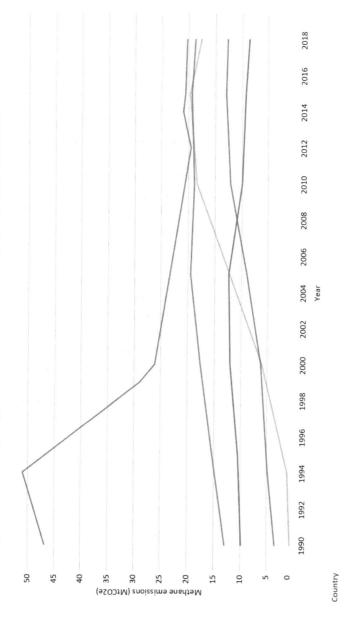

Source: World Resources Institute, "Climate Watch Historical GHG Emissions", 2021, https://www.climatewatchdata.org/ghg-emissions

solutions explored by countries in the past were not exclusively framed as methane abatement measures, but rather took the form of adaptation, public health, or carbon dioxide mitigation measures that have proven methane co-benefits.

Table 2 summarizes some of the measures pointed out by countries in their updated Nationally Determined Contributions (NDCs). It is evident that much of the methane-related abatement measures in the region focus on the waste and agriculture sectors, which is understandable as they are likely to have significant co-benefits in both adaptation and mitigation.[63] For instance, Cambodia and Myanmar both highlighted rice-cultivation measures as adaptation actions for climate resilience, but Cambodia also acknowledged the associated mitigation co-benefits. Recognizing and assessing such potential mitigation co-benefits (including methane abatement) in existing adaptation measures could assist countries in meeting and increasing their climate ambition. Meanwhile, abatement measures in the oil and gas sector are lacking in the NDCs. The countries' energy-related pledges are dominated by the development of new alternatives (such as renewables and low-carbon transport) and energy efficiency, rather than targeting existing facilities in the oil and gas sector. While this is appropriate for both short- and long-term low carbon development, methane abatement in the oil and gas sector can still play a role in the drastic and immediate emissions reductions needed up to 2030 (the period covered by current NDCs); especially since oil and gas are expected to grow, not shrink, in ASEAN up to 2035[64] and any phase-out is unlikely.

---

[63] Ayyoob Sharifi, "Co-Benefits and Synergies between Urban Climate Change Mitigation and Adaptation Measures: A Literature Review", *Science of the Total Environment* 750 (1 January 2021): 141642, https://doi.org/10.1016/j. scitotenv.2020.141642; Prabhakar Sivapuram, "Mitigation Co-Benefits of Adaptation Actions in Agriculture: An Opportunity for Promoting Climate Smart Agriculture in Indonesia", 2013, https://doi.org/10.3850/S1793924012100134

[64] ASEAN Centre for Energy, "ASEAN Plan of Action for Energy Cooperation (APAEC) Phase I: 2016–2025", ASEAN Centre for Energy, Jakarta, 2015.

Table 2: Targets and Measures in NDCs (Planned and/or Implemented) Relevant to Methane Abatement

Agriculture	Oil and Gas	Waste
Brunei		
		Reduce municipal waste to landfills to 1kg/person/day by 2035
Cambodia		
Emissions reduction of 6.2 MtCO2e (22.9 per cent reduction)	Emissions reduction of 13.7 MtCO2e (39.8 per cent reduction) in the energy sector	Emissions reduction of 0.6 MtCO2e (18.2 per cent reduction)
Development of rice crops and capacity building for increased climate resilience with mitigation co-benefits		Construction of 1,500 bio-digesters per year
		Improved management of industrial wastewater in the food and beverage sector
Indonesia		
Manure management for biogas in up to 0.06 per cent of cattle population in 2030		Landfill gas recovery enhancement

continued on next page

Table 2 — cont'd

Agriculture	Oil and Gas	Waste
Indonesia		
Feed supplement for cattle in up to 2.5 per cent of cattle population in 2030		Methane capture and utilization in industrial wastewater treatment
Laos		
Adjustment of water practices in lowland rice cultivation (50,000 hectares)		Reduction of 40 ktCO2e/yr in the waste sector
		Sustainable municipal solid waste management capacity of 500 tons/day in Vientiane
Malaysia		
—	—	—
Myanmar		
		Avoidance of 144 MtCO2e from 2030 BAU
		Reduce solid waste in landfills and implement landfill gas capture techniques and repurpose of organic waste

Philippines	—	—	—
Thailand	—	—	—
Singapore	—	—	—
Vietnam	Emissions reduction of 3.5 per cent compared to BAU (32.6 MtCO2e)	Emissions reduction of 16.7 per cent compared to BAU (155.8 MtCO2e) (energy sector)	Emissions reduction of 3.6 per cent compared to BAU (33.2 MtCO2e)
Use of short-duration rice varieties			
Alternating wet and dry irrigation			
Integrated crop management			
Improving rice growing models			
Improving diets for milk cows			
Collection and treatment of livestock organic waste			

Note: Shaded cells show sector-wide emissions reduction targets. White cells show specific mitigation actions relevant to methane. Conditional targets/measures were used where applicable.

Based on IPCC modelling, analysts have estimated that a median of 34 per cent reduction in methane emissions by 2030 is required for a 1.5-degree pathway.[65] In its new policy toolkit for engaging oil and gas producers on methane abatement, the IEA argues that voluntary industry-led efforts on methane are not enough to achieve the reductions required; government policy and regulation are critical in addressing barriers relating to information, infrastructure and investment.[66]

COLLABORATION AT THE ASEAN LEVEL

Besides subregional collaboration, existing ASEAN working groups in relevant sectors can also engage with climate experts and officials to expand their scope to cover methane abatement. These include the ASEAN Working Group on Chemicals and Waste, the ASEAN Working Group on Crops (which has already promoted Alternate Wetting and Drying techniques as part of rice intensification strategies),[67] the ASEAN Working Group on Livestock, and the Regional Energy Policy and Planning Sub-Sector Network (REPP-SNN), whose strategies include information sharing on the energy-climate nexus.[68]

Ultimately, both national and regional institutions can work with the private sector to make progress on methane. In 2021, Malaysia's PETRONAS hosted the inaugural ASEAN Energy Sector Methane Roundtable with representatives from the private sector and international

---

[65] Matthew J. Gidden et al., "The Global Methane Pledge and 1.5°C" (Climate Analytics, 12 April 2019).

[66] International Energy Agency, "Driving Down Methane Leaks from the Oil and Gas Industry", IEA, Paris, 2021, https://www.iea.org/reports/driving-down-methane-leaks-from-the-oil-and-gas-industry

[67] GIZ, "Alternate Wetting and Drying for Climate Change Adaptation, Mitigation and Livelihoods" (GIZ, Jakarta, 2021), https://asean-crn.org/wp-content/uploads/2021/06/Full-Brief_02_AWD_Paper-Series_June-2021.pdf

[68] APAEC Drafting Committee et al., "ASEAN Plan Of Action For Energy Cooperation (Apaec) 2016–2025 Phase II: 2021–2025" (ASEAN Centre for Energy (ACE) Jakarta, 2020).

organizations such as the IEA, World Bank and UNEP.[69] As a regional institution, ASEAN can play a role in future discourse while encouraging the regional private sector to play a more active role in international methane initiatives such as the OGMP 2.0.

BETTER DATA FOR STRONGER ACTION

While knowledge and data on methane emissions are growing as countries pay greater attention to its role in climate action, any meaningful policy measures would benefit from more granular data. Country reports of greenhouse gas emissions to the UNFCCC, which were used to construct the datasets cited in this paper and which provided the most consistent available data on historical country methane emissions, have been found to underestimate methane emissions when compared to atmospheric measurements.[70] In particular, the IEA has estimated that actual methane emissions from the oil and gas sector are about 70 per cent higher than what national governments report globally, and has now called for stronger monitoring efforts.[71] In the agriculture sector, reported methane emissions from rice cultivation are still difficult to verify using satellite data.

It is also critical to bear in mind that the tallied methane emissions consist of both actual measurement and modelling estimates. Within the estimates, there are assumptions made about the type and level of economic activities. As our understanding of the informal economies in Laos, Cambodia and Myanmar improves, a different pattern of emissions behaviours could emerge. Without benchmarking the implication of missing data in the region, it is important to be cautious when interpreting

---

[69] Petronas.com, "PETRONAS, Key ASEAN Energy Players To Intensify Collaboration In Addressing Methane Emissions", 27 October 2021, https://www.petronas.com/media/press-release/petronas-key-asean-energy-players-intensify-collaboration-addressing-methane (accessed 25 April 2022).

[70] Zhu Deng et al., "Comparing National Greenhouse Gas Budgets Reported in UNFCCC Inventories against Atmospheric Inversions", *Earth System Science Data Discussions*, 13 August 2021, pp. 1–59, https://doi.org/10.5194/essd-2021-235

[71] IEA, "Global Methane Tracker 2022 – Analysis".

marginal differences in statistical estimates of emissions. Nevertheless, the key insights in this paper are based on marked trends, which provide directions for accelerating action on key sources of methane in each country.

Further action on methane abatement, such as the formulation of national or sector-wide strategies, monitoring of progress towards country targets, and possibly the use of green finance in methane abatement projects, will require verified data at higher resolutions. Hence, the development and uptake of common reporting frameworks and databases such as the International Methane Emissions Observatory for both national and company inventories would be one potential area for closer international cooperation on methane.

CONCLUSION

As calls strengthen for an urgent ramp-up in global climate action, targeting methane emissions can help achieve the rapid reductions in greenhouse gas emissions needed by 2030 to keep the world on track for 1.5 degrees of warming.

ASEAN countries have an important role to play in this process.

While methane comes from a variety of sectors and therefore demands a variety of approaches, ASEAN countries can be placed into groups depending on which sectors they need to focus on. For instance, Indonesia, Malaysia and Singapore have the common goal of tackling methane emissions from the waste sector. Identifying countries in the region that face similar challenges can spur collaboration and knowledge sharing on the kind of policy changes needed to push for emissions reduction in specific sectors.

In agricultural sectors like rice cultivation and livestock, reducing methane emissions is associated with adaptation co-benefits such as greater climate resilience, although the effectiveness and feasibility of solutions are uncertain so far. On the other hand, solutions for methane abatement in the oil and gas sector are clearer and offer proven policy options and a greater understanding of cost and feasibility at the country level. ASEAN countries, especially Brunei and Malaysia. stand to achieve significant methane reduction as well as cost savings in this sector.

As data collection and emission modelling improve, greater cooperation at the subregional level can help countries tackle their specific obstacles, while cooperation at the ASEAN level can make use of existing institutional structures to prioritize methane abatement.

Annex 1: Estimated Abatement Costs and Potential in the Asia-Pacific Oil and Gas Sector, by Technology

Production Source	Abatement Technology	Cost (US$/ MBtu)	Possible Savings (kt)
Downstream gas	Downstream LDAR	−79	1,596
	Install flares	3	49
	Replace with electric motor	−59	204
	Replace with instrument air systems	−134	11
	Vapour recovery units	−31	5
	Other	−32	326
Downstream oil	Downstream LDAR	−79	13
	Install flares	112	8
	Vapour recovery units	−31	6
Offshore gas	Install flares	17	301
	Replace compressor seal or rod	−106	0
	Replace with instrument air systems	−116	29
	Upstream LDAR	−321	225
	Vapour recovery units	−90	63
Offshore oil	Install flares	16	258
	Replace compressor seal or rod	−98	0
	Replace with instrument air systems	−107	24
	Upstream LDAR	−289	39
	Vapour recovery units	−166	196
Offshore conventional gas	Blowdown capture	−100	100
	Early replacement of devices	−1	20
	Install flares	23	3

	Install plunger	−66	10
	Replace pumps	−107	41
	Replace with electric motor	−47	162
	Replace with instrument air systems	−73	224
	Upstream LDAR	−317	367
	Vapour recovery units	−21	10
Onshore conventional oil	Blowdown capture	−116	0
	Early replacement of devices	−3	28
	Install flares	83	6
	Replace pumps	−93	59
	Replace with electric motor	36	406
	Replace with instrument air systems	−80	170
	Upstream LDAR	−351	84
	Vapour recovery units	−133	194
	Other	2	8
Unconventional gas	Blowdown capture	−48	53
	Early replacement of devices	3	11
	Install flares	19	1
	Install plunger	−30	5
	Replace pumps	−51	22
	Replace with electric motor	−21	87
	Replace with instrument air systems	−34	121
	Upstream LDAR	−146	197
	Vapour recovery units	−7	5
Unconventional oil	Vapour recovery units	−15	0

Source: International Energy Agency (IEA), "Global Methane Tracker 2022 – Analysis", https://www.iea.org/reports/global-methane-tracker-2022 (accessed 10 March 2022).